LIBRARY TRAINING GUIDES

Series Editor: David Baker
Editorial Assistant: Joan Welsby

LIBRARY TRAINING GUIDES

Training needs analysis

Michael Williamson

Library Association Publishing

© Library Association Publishing Ltd 1993

Published by
Library Association Publishing Ltd
7 Ridgmount Street
London WC1E 7AE

First published 1993

British Library Cataloguing in Publication Data. A catalogue record for this book is available from the British Library.

ISBN 1-85604-077-1

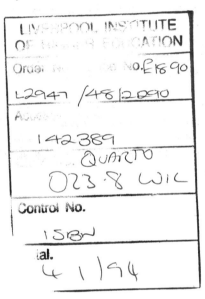
Typeset in 11/12pt Palermo by Library Association Publishing Ltd
Printed and made in Great Britain by Amber (Printwork) Ltd, Harpenden, Herts.

Introduction by the Series Editor

This new series of Library Training Guides (LTGs for short) aims to fill the gap left by the demise of the old Training Guidelines published in the 1980s in the wake of the Library Association's work on staff training. The new LTGs develop the original concept of concisely written summaries of the best principles and practice in specific areas of training by experts in the field which give library and information workers a good-quality guide to best practice. Like the original guidelines, the LTGs also include appropriate examples from a variety of library systems as well as further reading and useful contacts.

Though each guide stands in its own right, LTGs form a coherent whole. Acquisition of all LTGs as they are published will result in a comprehensive manual of training and staff development in library and information work.

The guides are aimed at practising librarians and library training officers. They are intended to be comprehensive without being over-detailed; they should give both the novice and the experienced librarian/training officer an overview of what should/could be done in a given situation and in relation to a particular skill/group of library staff/type of library.

David Baker

Contents

Introduction

The broad aim of this guide is to present an introduction to training needs analysis (TNA) in all its many forms and to relate this process specifically to library training.

The term 'training needs analysis' has a rather technical ring about it; a phrase that might have originated in America? Something to do with corporate management and the rather obscure jargon of 'big business'? A simple enough concept to understand, perhaps, but something that has little to do with the everyday life of the library trainer, who has probably already got too much to contend with trying to cope with regular cutbacks and reorganizations, the financial demands of the cost unit and the recurring problems of a recession which may or may not be going away?

Of course everybody will readily agree that training is a very good thing. This was something that was instilled into us all at an early stage in our professional development. We know that we need to provide training when faced with the introduction of new technology. We turn to training when new developments come along and remember to include it within our action plans. 'Management of change' courses are always useful to counter the approach of yet another restructuring exercise, and we all suspect or can prove that a customer care programme will be beneficial to our staff and will show that we are at the forefront of current thinking. Some of us may be lucky enough to be able to draw on the central training services of our organizations, particularly within the field of management development.

Training funds can be at risk during times of economic restraint and we must always ensure that every activity that we are engaged in is giving good value for money. We know that planning and forethought are sensible but everybody is always looking for the convenient shortcut.

A 'training plan' for our organization can often, therefore, be an ideal which is never realized; something which we will prepare when other matters have been taken care of and everything has settled down? Something which we have but admit that it is out-of-date following the recent re-evaluation of the service? Something which we never really feel that we can justify spending the time on and for which we are always ready with valid excuses?

If comprehensive, up-to-date training plans for organizations are difficult to find within the field of librarianship, how much more unlikely is it that we will find that these plans have been drawn up using the sound principles of TNA?

A number of librarians have commented that they are suspicious of the planning process within training. There seems to be a general feeling of being so busy that managers would rather plunge in at the deep end and get on with what training can be afforded without any of the preliminaries. Many believe that they inherently know what is required and would rather get on with it. In times of restraint these feelings are understandable but can also be very dangerous. While personal intuition can often play an important part in the identification of training need, it can also be used as a smokescreen – an excuse for sticking to tried and tested programmes and for avoiding new developments.

This guide seeks to explain TNA in simple terms and to describe how it can be used to create an adaptable and effective training plan for any library organization. It aims to identify all the advantages of a fully analytical approach to the training process. Methods of identifying the training needs of both individuals and organizations will be considered and will be directly related to the formation of effective library training programmes. The guide is as practical as possible and includes examples of good practice within the appendices.

Throughout the guide reference is made to 'library trainer', a term which should be taken to mean the member of staff with the management responsibility for training within any library system. Realistically, training officers will not be found in all organizations.

Thanks are due to all of the library systems who have provided examples of current training plans and training analysis forms.

 # TNA: a broad definition

'Training needs analysis is the systematic approach to determining the real training needs which exist within an organization or department.'

Definitions are sometimes questionable and often create as many problems as they solve. Unfortunately, many of us pick up the catchword of the moment and adapt it slightly to suit our needs. In this way terms can become confusing.

While collecting information for this guide, it was possible to examine the training programmes of many different library organizations. From these documents it became clear that TNA can be interpreted in two different ways. Some managers will refer to it as the complete process of identifying the basic training needs and then following all the necessary steps until these needs have been analysed and addressed in the best possible way. The pure interpretation of the term describes the final process only. This guide uses the former definition in order to clarify all the elements of the chain.

Although interpretation can vary, it is important that there should be consistency of practice within any organization and all staff should be fully aware of the meaning of local terminology in this field. In particular the term 'training need' can be applied in a vague way which can produce undesirable results.

Library trainers who embark on a full programme of TNA will need to be meticulous and will wish to relate findings to actual performance and its implications. They will try not to be influenced by existing opinions, current practice or the pressures of the moment. They will want to have a clear idea of what they mean by TNA and will need to be able to interpret this successfully to others. Some basic definitions follow.

1.1 Training need

When we talk about *'training need'* we usually mean that we have identified a need for an improvement or change in performance either by an individual or by a group of staff within an organization.

It is always important to remember that not all *'performance needs'* will necessarily be solved by the provision of training. There might be other alternatives. Poor performance could be related to poor working conditions, for example, or a lack of motivation. Training is an expensive solution to 'performance need' and should always be fully justified.

If we can identify clearly that this particular 'need' can be met by a training solution than a 'training need' is born. 'Training need', therefore, can be simply defined as *'a need for performance improvement or change which can best be met by training of some kind'*.

1.2 Identification of training need

This involves the process or processes we choose in order fully to identify and define the training needs within our organization. These can be the needs of individual members of staff or can relate to the organization itself. These should be complementary but may be very different.

This process will involve specific skills and techniques. It is necessary to ensure that one can distinguish clearly between genuine 'needs' and personal wishes. It should be possible to differentiate between the need for tasks and skills and development training and to be aware of the relationship between them.

During this stage it is important to establish clearly which of the identified 'performance needs' are actual 'training needs' and which might be addressed in other ways.

1.3 Analysis of training need

Having identified the training needs, careful analysis must take place in order to establish how exactly these needs can be met. This process will involve a detailed examination of the needs and the library trainer will want to consider such matters as cost, resources, organizational priorities and time-scale.

The complete process of TNA will involve all of these different elements and will also have an influence upon the other stages within the training cycle. Some trainers believe that 'Performance Needs Analysis' is a more appropriate description of the whole exercise which can be simply described as follows:

- We should be attempting to identify those discrepancies or problems with performance and achievement within our organizations.
- We should be considering any gaps which may exist between what staff are actually doing and what they should be doing; what they are capable of doing and what may be needed from them in the future.
- We should be able to identify which of these needs can be solved by training.
- We should be able to look at the training needs identified and establish how best these needs might be met, given the current situation and local conditions within our particular organization.

Successful TNA demands determination and attention to detail. The cry of 'no skills; no time and no resources' may soon be heard, but a targeted training policy based on sound analytical principles will quickly begin to demonstrate economic sense when compared with more traditional, reactive methods.

It would be very easy to allow the whole process to work in reverse and to find that training is being undertaken in an *ad hoc* way. The result of this is likely to be that training will be provided which

- is not required
- is not made use of
- is too late or too early to be of any use
- is always last year's programme which steadily becomes more and more irrelevant
- recognizes the 'it's your turn this year' principle
- is not good value for money

A competent trainer should always have a clear understanding of the definition of terms and will always keep them in mind. Good training, the need for which has been carefully analysed, will always result in:

- An improved image
- A better service for our users
- Improved motivation among our staff
- More able and competent staff
- A more cost-effective service

2 TNA: its place within the training framework

Tradition and practice

A broad process has now been identified which seems to fit neatly into the first segments of the traditional training cycle. Most trainers will be familiar with the following types of continuous sequence:

- Establish organizational aims
- Identify training needs
- Plan training
- Deliver training
- Evaluate training

Evaluation will inevitably lead to change, either by fine tuning or by the adoption of new methods and by the revision of objectives and the identification of more need. Thus the activity comes full circle and one is ready to undertake TNA once more. This continuous process should be well known but it may often seem that most of the time and effort will be expended on the delivery of the training without too much concern for a scientific approach towards needs analysis. While this may be understandable, for the reasons given earlier, the ultimate success of the training will depend upon the first sections of the cycle being completed accurately. The situation may also be aggravated by trainers being unwilling or unable to address the evaluation process properly. In such cases the result is often 'training for the sake of training', training in itself having been identified as a good thing. This can be the worst possible scenario, particularly from an economic point of view. All training is expensive. All training must be justified.

In effect, of course, training needs are being agreed in many arbitrary ways. Having a general preconception that all training must be good, the library trainer may identify it naturally in one or more of the following ways:

1 From course programmes which are circulated to the organization. A programme which appears relevant may generate a nomination.
    In an organization where there is no formal training plan this can be a very expensive form of training and can produce very unbalanced results.
2 By the reliance on a central training programme. Many local authorities provide good centralized management development training and offer courses to all departments.
    Again, where no formal policy or plan exists for the library system, the courses are not likely to be as effective as they might be.
3 By responding to the individual requests of staff, who may be left to seek their own programmes.
    Very unbalanced results will ensue. There will be a tendency for the

organization to respond to 'wants', not 'needs'.

4 By individual decision and determination of the library trainer, the chief librarian or any kind of senior management team.

In some cases this must be inevitable but if it is to be the only criterion it will fail to address many issues.

A survey of library organizations within the United Kingdom suggests a very unbalanced approach to training. Some have devised complex published training plans, based on clear aims and objectives, on which are founded a whole variety of training programmes and policies. Others have restricted themselves to looking for training from elsewhere and tend to accept whatever may be available.

The most familiar programmes provided seem to be planned for induction. Most organizations seem to have clearly identified general induction as a training need.

The second most common programmes to be found are the Approved Programmes prepared for the Library Association as part of the professional qualification process. It is interesting to note how this requirement has begun to improve the quality of training in the workplace. Library trainers have been obliged to prepare comprehensive programmes with specific reference to particular aims and objectives. Unfortunately, the programmes will usually be designed to apply only to particular staff members. Reactive TNA can, therefore, sometimes produce good results. However, it should not need much consideration to understand that this may equally not be the case. All training undertaken must be generated from some kind of awareness of need. Bad TNA will do much to negate the benefits of any subsequent training. This in itself will have a direct effect on those being trained and, of course, must raise the question of 'value for money'.

2.2 Cost implications

We should all be fully aware of the considerable cost of training. Sometimes, if an identifiable training fund is provided within the budget of an organization there will be a tendency for expenditure to take place without too much concern for profitable outcome. Again, training is being considered as good in itself. The fund may pay for a certain number of people to attend a specific number of courses and library trainers may consider that they have fulfilled their function of good financial management if the fund is still within the budget at the end of the financial year. It is because of this common attitude towards training funds that they often become vulnerable in times of financial difficulties.

Of course, the cost of bad training, or badly identified training, will reflect on other elements of the library budget. The salaries of participants attending training programmes will be a significant consideration but to this must also be added the probable costs of travelling, subsistence, administration, materials etc. If the training involved does not really meet the needs of the library system concerned, the costs jump alarmingly. Poorly conceived or executed training could cost an organization many thousands of pounds.

The only way to have truly cost-effective training is to make sure that it is based on solid TNA. This means careful research and analysis within the library system before any training is actually carried out. This also requires development of a sound understanding of the concept of a training need and of the whole TNA process.

2.3 TNA: the process

In an ideal situation, an organization will always be examining the performance of staff and this will naturally contribute towards TNA. Sometimes major changes, such as the introduction of new technology or a restructuring proposal, will raise questions about performance which will also help to identify need. In such a situation the trainer will need to be sensitive to the mood of the organization. The best TNA takes place in an atmosphere of mutual cooperation between managers, trainers and staff.

Turning again to the 'training cycle' with particular reference to the first three processes (i.e. the fuller interpretation of TNA), one will find that it is possible to break down the process into more detail and the new sequence can be summarized as follows:

- Establishment of organizational aims and objectives
- Alertness for possible problems in performance
- Identified concern about performance
- Identification of training needs
- Analysis of training needs
- Setting of training objectives
- Final completion of training plan

It may be useful to examine these broad headings in more detail.

2.3.1 Establishment of organizational aims and objectives

All training must originate from the aims and objectives of the organization itself. It must not be an end in itself but should, in some way, be contributing towards the achievement of these objectives. Some organizations will not have formal written statements of objectives and, in other cases, these may be consolidated in a very brief statement which may obscure some of the meaning. The library trainer may find it necessary to clarify aims and objectives before the work of analysis can truly begin. This should not be a difficult task but one must be very clear about why a particular library organization exists. Who are the users? What are their needs? What are the corporate needs of the organization?

Within any organization there will be a need to plan for the future. Many will be familiar with business plans which include statements about the type of activity to be aimed for, the level of activity to be achieved and the resources needed to support these activities. Eventually trainers will be comparing what has actually occurred with what was planned to occur, with the monitoring and evaluating process taking place either during the activity or immediately following it. One will thus be able to analyse and investigate any possible gap between the planned level of activity and the actual level to see if it can be established why the organization did not perform as well as planned.

Corporate aims and objectives are relatively easy to establish. If they are not formally recorded the library trainer will be fully aware of them and should be able to relate training needs directly to them.

Problems may begin to occur when one attempts to analyse the corporate structure in more detail. It is desirable that one examines the purpose of the work of individual members of staff and groups of staff working within the organization and, as a result, is able to understand how these secondary objectives form a part of the corporate objectives as a whole.

Some of these questions may be readily answerable but it will always be better to involve the staff themselves in these discussions.

2.3.2 Alertness for possible problems in performance

Once completely aware of the aims and objectives of the library system (and perhaps how these fit within the more general aims of a larger, containing organization) one must be vigilant in order to identify how possible problems with performance may be interfering with the achievement of these aims and objectives. In a very small system this might simply be a question of good communication skills and constant alertness on the part of the library trainer and staff. In a larger system this will not be practicable and a more formal process will need to be introduced.

2.3.3 Identified concern about performance

Once an organization has alerted itself to the possibility of problems in performance, specific problems may begin to appear. Many large organizations now operate some kind of *performance management system* based on the detailed, analysed job descriptions of their staff. This can be related directly to broad aims and objectives and detailed business plans. In effect an early warning system is being set up which can indicate when need of any kind occurs. Full TNA can be incorporated within such a system.

Alternatively, when organizations are confronted with restructuring or change of any kind, they may choose to introduce a TNA process which is able to stand on its own. This type of process can involve all staff in research activity which may identify a wide range of performance need.

2.3.4 Identification of training needs

Having identified specific concerns about performance, the next step will be to decide how best the organization can revert to its performance objectives. Needs have been identified but there may be solutions other than training. A new air ventilation system, more effectively designed workstations or longer coffee breaks may, in fact, be more effective in solving our problems. It is at this stage, in particular, that the cost of a training solution should be borne in mind. Before a training need is established we must be absolutely sure that this is the right solution and that we are not overlooking obvious and simpler alternatives. Our objective is not to train for the sake of training but to train for performance improvement and the ultimate accomplishment of organizational and individual goals. At the end of this stage we should have identified specific 'training needs'.

2.3.5 Analysis of training needs

It is now possible to embark on a detailed analysis of how these needs should best be met. This will involve particular skills and abilities.

In addition to examining the specific need it will be important to consider its relationship to all the relevant surrounding factors. Important considerations such as practicality, cost, learning issues involved and the current priorities of the organization will all have to be investigated. At this stage it will be helpful to begin to group needs together within logical hierarchies and clusters. A series of interviews with individuals may produce a pattern of emerging need which can ultimately be addressed from a cooperative point of view while, of course, the 'one-off' individual need will also have to be dealt with.

2.3.6   Setting of training objectives

The next step involves translating the training needs so identified into training aims and objectives – succinct but understandable summaries of what we are setting out to achieve. It is at this stage that all training needs begin to be broken down and grouped into manageable areas. This is the first stage in the preparation of a full training business plan for the library system.

Initially, it will probably be useful to group the needs into the three principal fields of training:

- Induction training
- Tasks and skills training
- Development training

Within these broad groupings it will always be important to identify levels of staff concerned and the way in which the training is to be provided.

2.3.7   Final completion of training plan

The final training plan should set down the full training needs of the organization in an understandable and manageable way. One ought to be able to see exactly:

- Who is going to be trained?
- What are they going to be trained in?
- What method is going to be used?
- The timescale (when applicable)
- Who is going to be responsible for the training?
- What resources and support are available?
- The ultimate objectives

The final creation of the training plan is only the beginning of the task. Training needs will always be changing and developing. When the training is actually put into operation it should always be assessed and evaluated, and this information should find its way back to the start of the cycle again, influencing the future identification of training needs.

The next part of the Guide examines in more detail the processes involved in the identification of training needs.

3 Identification of training need

Work within this area may be divided neatly into *corporate training needs* and *individual training needs*. Many corporate needs identified will have a direct bearing on the individual, while the specific needs of individuals may build up into a major corporate need. However, it will generally be helpful to consider both areas separately when undertaking any investigation. Before examining the two areas in more detail it is essential to understand what *training aids* or *sources* may be available. These can be defined as follows:

3.1 Training aids and sources

- Training budgets
- Organizational charts and structures
- Written aims and objectives/business plans
- Job descriptions/person specifications
- Personnel/training records
- Staff appraisal/performance management documents
- Complaints from users
- Questionnaires
- Direct observation/self-observation
- Interviews

Where these sources or possibilities exist it will always be useful for the library trainer to become familiar with them before undertaking any analysis work. Each can provide invaluable help during the identification of need process.

3.1.1 *Training budgets*

Some library systems have no training budget at all. Others have funds which can only be used for training fees but which may be supplemented from other areas of the budget (e.g. travelling and subsistence). Whatever the local situation may be, it will be important for the library trainer to be fully aware of all possible restraints and limitations before commencing work. The resource base must have a considerable influence on the setting of priorities. With the advent of the local cost centre it may become increasingly likely that funds can be more easily transferred from one budget head to another if priorities can be demonstrated. The process and possible implications of this must be fully understood. It is also becoming increasingly common for managers with central training responsibilities to be placed in the position of providing training for a variety of local cost centres, each with their own list of priorities and budget allocation.

3.1.2 | *Organizational charts and structures*

This leads naturally to the necessity of being fully aware of current structures within the organization. This is a straightforward exercise but one which may be complicated by devolvement and the requirement for cost centres to adjust and adapt according to demand. The library trainer must not only be aware of current structures and potential differences between clients but also must be alert to the possibility of change within any area. The charts available should show detailed substructures and the direct relationships between all members of staff.

3.1.3 | *Written aims and objectives/business plans*

These will be an essential tool for the library trainer, particularly during corporate analysis. It has already been noted that, in some cases, aims and objectives may not be recorded formally and that we may need to confirm them. In other systems detailed business plans may state broad and specific objectives for a defined time-scale into the future. These may relate to individual cost units or specific libraries or departments within larger systems. In an ideal situation, the training unit itself will be working towards the achievement of its own business plan. Whatever the local situation, and however large the organization concerned, the library trainer must collect or create comprehensive data within this area.

3.1.4 | *Job descriptions/person specifications*

Job descriptions are statements of the purpose, responsibilities and tasks which constitute a particular job. They are now a basic management tool but their value will be lessened if they are too general in content. They should help to clarify job content and will assist with job evaluation, staff development and performance management exercises.

Person specifications will provide details about the sort of person who will be most qualified to fill a particular post. They will refer to length of experience necessary, appropriate qualifications and desirable personal abilities and attributes. Person specifications will be particularly useful during the selection and recruitment process.

Many library systems now have job descriptions and person specifications for all their posts and, obviously, the information contained within these documents will be vital to the library trainer. Unfortunately, changes take place within organizations on a regular basis and amendments to job descriptions tend to lag behind. If these are sources which are to be relied upon heavily then their currency must be questioned and maintained. These sources provide the detail which is usually missing from broad organizational charts. They may clarify the hierarchy and responsibility issues and should give clear guidance for the identification of practical tasks and skills training needs.

The library trainer may wish to use these documents as a direct link between skills required and training provided, but some process will be necessary to ensure that the member of staff is not already fully trained within a particular area of need. Job descriptions and person specifications will always be useful in setting training objectives.

3.1.5 Personnel/training records

An effective training unit will wish to record details of all training undertaken and, when we are dealing with identification of need, it will be important to be aware of what has been tried before and how successful it was. The general monitoring and evaluation of training can contribute towards the re-identification of need but it will be essential also to be aware of the particular circumstances of the individual. Some elements of the personnel records may not be available to the library trainer but, if true identification of training need is to take place, it will be vital for at least some of this information to be shared. Many systems now maintain comprehensive training records on each member of staff. These may be filed separately from the main personnel file, or be an accessible part of the main record. They will contain information about what training has been provided for or undertaken by an individual and may suggest a pattern of need. Where such records are held centrally it will be essential for them to be as up-to-date as possible. Ideally they should record the date of the training, some indication of the result, and any follow-up action considered desirable.

There may be other information contained within the personnel files which could indicate training need. This may seem particularly to be the case with information about possible disciplinary action but there will usually be better ways by which this kind of need can be spotted. The separation of general historical training information from the main file will probably be the most useful action which can be taken here.

3.1.6 Staff appraisal/performance management documents

In an organization where a formal staff appraisal or performance management scheme is in operation, the library trainer should easily be able to obtain additional information on training needs required. Again, confidentiality may be an important concern but the trainer will only be interested in a particular element of the information being produced and a good scheme will provide for this. Generally, current training needs will be discussed and agreed between member of staff and immediate supervisor during the regular interview. This information may be recorded on to a separate page which could then be forwarded to the library trainer or, alternatively, a copy of the relevant section can be provided. Most forms of this kind are not designed to include detail about the different kinds of need but rather leave sufficient space for any need to be expressed. This will always be a useful way of collecting and possibly combining perceived individual training need.

3.1.7 Complaints from users

It is becoming increasingly common for the library trainer to have access to information about user complaints. Following the introduction of the Customer Charter there has been a tendency for complaints to be collected in a more formal way. Forms will probably be provided at all service points and users will be positively encouraged to make their feelings known.
Many trainers shrink from relying too heavily on such forms when identifying need and certainly there will be a need for caution. It is easy to dismiss individual complaints as the perversity of human nature and to reassure ourselves that, if the majority of our users do not echo the complaint, it

was probably a false alarm. However, in reality, our users may very well be more accurate and valid observers of need than our own colleagues and we should be particularly alert for any pattern emerging from the information we receive.

3.1.8 *Questionnaires*

Asking other people to complete forms, in order to explain how they perceive training need, is a tried and traditional method which we should consider in some detail. We may choose to prepare a general form which could require all members of staff to list their current opinions about personal need or we may decide to make it more specific in order to test our effectiveness in particular areas.

There are standard questionnaires and printed psychological tests available on the market which may be useful in determining the attitudes, personality, aptitude or educational achievement of members of staff. In certain situations, and from a general point of view, these may be useful but it is probable that a form which has been designed internally for local purposes will provide much better and more relevant information.

Designing your own questionnaire is not a difficult task but, before undertaking it, there are various points to remember:

- Ensure that your questionnaire is fully recognized as having the full backing of the organization. To make sure of this, it is probably useful to introduce your questions briefly by referring to the management decision which generated the research.
- Make sure that the questions you ask are presented in such a way that your intended respondents will understand fully what information you seek.
- Use a style and language which your respondents will understand.
- Always keep the wording of the questionnaire positive.
- Restrict the questions you are asking to a manageable number. It is sensible to ask no more than 20 questions and to plan for the questionnaire to be completed easily within 30 minutes.
- Make your questions as specific as possible and check to make sure that all of the answers will provide you with useful information.
- Avoid asking questions about facts which you can easily find in other ways (i.e. by consulting printed information).
- Be straightforward in your approach. Don't play tricks on your respondents or set any traps for them.
- Break questions down to their simplest form. Try not to ask any multiple questions (two or more questions in one) or combine ideas which may be mutually exclusive. This will be particularly important when you are seeking yes/no answers.
- Take some trouble with the layout of your questionnaire. Present your questions in an attractive and understandable way. Separate questions so that they can be read easily and leave sufficient space for answers.
- Whenever possible, try to have a test run with any new questionnaire which you are planning to use. Try to involve any staff who may be going to help in the collection of information or testing procedures. Be prepared to reconsider and redesign.
- Be very careful in your choice of respondents so that a consensus result will be meaningful. In particular, try to make sure that all your potential respondents are able to provide the information you require.

- If possible, avoid choosing respondents from among staff who may have some kind of vested interest in the result of the questionnaire. However well meaning they may be, it will be difficult to avoid inadvertent personal bias.
- Consider carefully whether or not you need staff to identify themselves personally. An anonymous reply may be acceptable and may encourage a more open response. If you feel that you do need to identify staff eventually, give some thought to the use of an identifying number to maintain an element of confidentiality.
- When dealing with a specific group of staff, try to include all members of the group to make sure that the quality of the result is high. If this should not be possible for any reason take particular care in your choice of sample respondents and establish that they are truly representative of the target group. The main criteria for choice should be:

1 Is the member of staff a decision-maker or manager within the area of need being investigated?
2 Are they familiar with the current work procedures in the area of investigation?
3 Does the member of staff have any special subject knowledge which might be useful?
4 Is the member of staff someone who relates well to others in the section? Do they have the trust and commitment of their colleagues?

Questionnaires can usually be divided into two main types: 'closed' or 'controlled answer' questionnaires, or 'open' or 'free expression' ones. Obviously the type of question that you ask is going to have a major influence on your final results so considerable thought should be given to your decision.

The *closed* questionnaire will ask the following type of question and will provide a choice of basic answer for selection.

For example: *The red button should be pressed before the till will operate?*
True/False
I found the recent health and safety course relevant to my job.
Yes/No
I need more training in customer care. Yes/No

Respondents will be required to tick only one particular answer and this may be a useful type of questionnaire when you are trying to assess whether or not knowledge has been absorbed following a training programme. The results can be gathered together easily but may not provide a great deal of information. However, respondents are more likely to complete this type of questionnaire accurately and will generally return it promptly. Always remember to vary the true/false or yes/no answers so that a recognizable pattern does not develop.

The *open* questionnaire will invite the respondent to give a short statement or will require an essay type of answer.

For example: *Which of your tasks do you find most difficult?*
What health and safety training have you received?

If the respondents are willing to spend some time and trouble on their answers, this type of questionnaire may provide valuable information. In general, staff may be willing to open up and share their opinions, particularly in sensitive areas. However, such answers will take longer to read and the overall results will be more difficult to assess.

A common approach to the assessment of open questionnaires is to seek for 'key words' and phrases which may appear in more than one answer.

Priority ordering is a broader type of closed question which may ask the respondent to prioritize a sequence of statements or answers. This can be useful as long as the sequence does not become too long and unwieldy.

For example: You could ask a member of staff to arrange a sequence of ten tasks in order of frequency or perceived difficulty.

Rating scales may also be helpful when you want the respondent to indicate the extent to which they agree or disagree with a fixed statement.

For example: *I do not require any technical skills in order to undertake my job.* Strongly agree/Agree/Not sure/Disagree/Strongly disagree

You may very well want to force your respondent into expressing an opinion, in which case the 'not sure' response is not going to be particularly useful. There will always be a tendency for respondents to select the middle choice so, if you require a definite result, it is usually best to provide an even number of options. Whenever you are preparing a rating scale you should take care to vary the position of the responses on the scale and consider the use of alternative terminology for some of the responses.

For example: understand/don't understand
positive/negative
enthusiastic/unenthusiastic

This may help to avoid the tendency for some respondents to choose the same line throughout the questionnaire.

The results of most questionnaires can be presented in a tabulated form which will enable the library trainer to present a coordinated summary of their findings. This will be important for presentations and may enable the results to be analysed more readily.

Another important matter to consider will be the administration of the questionnaire. Sending it to individual members of staff by post, with a covering letter, may be inevitable but this can produce late responses or no response at all. If possible, bring respondents together so that a personal presentation can be made and the need for the research can be fully explained. In this way time can be allowed for questions; one can also ensure that everybody understands exactly what they are being asked to do and responses can be collected immediately.

It would not be sensible to rely only on questionnaires when trying to identify training needs but they can often be used effectively as part of other research activities. Many will be used as the basis for personal interviews with all members of staff.

Two methods in particular can help to facilitate a more accurate collection of information through questionnaires: the *group method* and the *Delphi technique*.

1 The group method

This is a kind of controlled brainstorming and can be particularly useful with groups of staff whom you suspect may be reluctant or diffident about sharing their views openly. This process enables participants to express opinions anonymously in the first instance and can prevent the formulation of hasty conclusions. It involves the following stages:

- Identify and bring together a group of respondents (e.g. the staff of a particular library).
- Set objectives clearly (e.g. identification of training need within the particular library).
- Take the first question from your prepared questionnaire (e.g. *What do you feel are the most important training needs from your point of view*) and ask each member of the group to write down their answer. Allow no talking or collusion and set a short time limit (e.g. five minutes).
- Collect answers and record them on a board/flip chart. Indicate clearly where similar needs have been identified. Allow the group to examine answers and then repeat the exercise until all needs have been collected.
- Ask each member of the group to arrange all the identified needs into an order of perceived priority, again in isolation and in writing.
- Collate information. Remove needs which have a low priority and continue with the exercise until there is a consensus of defined need.
- Record final list of priorities and allow members of the group to comment in writing on the broad question and final result. Move on to the next question.
- Provide feedback for the group after the event.

This exercise provides a useful kind of workshop as it generally avoids the problem of one or two members of staff dominating a group response.

2 The Delphi technique

This process has many of the advantages of the group method but can be used for a greater number of people in different locations over a longer period of time.
The main steps are as follows:

- Prepare your questionnaire.
- Select your ideal group of respondents.
- Introduce the exercise clearly to all participants.
- Send out the questionnaire by post with a clear 'reply by' date.
- Receive replies and chase up late ones.
- Analyse responses and prepare a second questionnaire in order to refine and test the responses given.
- Repeat this process as many times as seems desirable until the responses have been fully expanded and developed.
- Provide feedback.

This is an especially useful exercise for a scattered, decentralized organization but it is important to keep the questionnaires brief.

Current library practice

Many examples of different kinds of questionnaires are already being used by library systems. This may help in the understanding of the different kinds of responses which each may generate (see Appendix 2).

A questionnaire which simply states: 'What do you consider to be your current training needs?', followed by a large space, will almost certainly result in limited answers unless it is administered under very controlled conditions. Forms of this kind are likely to produce a superficial reaction and it is probable that the member of staff will focus on a particular current concern. While useful data may be obtained it is unlikely that comprehensive need will be identified.

Some types of questionnaire are based on the principles of performance management while others ask general open questions about the individual's perception of need. Broad headings may be provided to give a firmer structure to the answers. These may specify tasks and skills needs/development needs/knowledge/attitude etc.

Other examples have used the training programme of the previous year as a starting point. Staff are asked to record which elements of the programme they found most useful and which areas they feel would be most helpful to them in the future. In such a form as this there is usually provision for the unforeseen answer which might, of course, be very important.

Suffolk Arts and Libraries Service began their TNA exercise by conducting a series of informal interviews with representative staff from different libraries who all had the job titles of library assistant, enquiry officer or library manager. In this way they were able to identify the core skills/knowledge, defined by basic statements, which were felt to be required to carry out these jobs effectively. Notes from these sessions were distributed back to those who had participated and also to their line managers, in order to try to identify any areas previously omitted and to gain some insight into the views of more senior staff. The final result was a list of statements which defined each job title.

This information determined the structure of the questionnaires. In order to help staff to assess themselves more accurately on their own knowledge and skill, it was felt that a series of core questions should be answered which would then lead to the appropriate statement. It was considered that this would also help to assess more exactly where the respondent felt that there was a lack of knowledge. This work produced three quite detailed individual questionnaires (one for each job title) which were then sent out to all the relevant staff, who were required to make very specific responses.

Another approach is to list all possible tasks and duties against every individual level of staff who might be expected to undertake such work. Staff are then asked to identify areas of need set against the full range of work being undertaken within the organization. This is an excellent approach as it can force staff to make choices and encourages them to make comments against all elements of their jobs. The collective information received can also be used corporately to undertake a comprehensive *training audit*. This term is used to describe the process of comparing current training provision against total organizational training need. This type of detailed research is perhaps more likely to be found in larger organizations where there is some need for uniformity of approach across the board. It will also be vital when more than one organization or department is involved.

The work recently initiated by the Northern Training Group with funding from the Public Library Development Initiative Scheme used a similar kind of process. The first phase of this project set out to establish the priority training needs of ten individual authorities, for which adequate training provision was not available and which could justify investment in open learning materials. The TNA approach was competence based and comprehensive. Five broad job contexts were identified which covered all jobs within libraries apart from chief officers and deputies (e.g. library assistant, functional manager etc.).

Questionnaires were devised, piloted at a workshop, and then administered by the individual authorities. The information collected was entered on a database and the results were verified and reviewed at workshops. A training audit was also undertaken and it then became a simple matter to compare current training need with current training provision (see Appendix 1).

Although the task may appear to be a large one, the concept is very good as the library trainer will need to identify and break down all organizational functions and staff responsibilities when preparing the final training plan. To undertake the exercise at this earlier stage can only be advantageous. The provision of a *functional map* may help to facilitate the production of comprehensive questionnaires and should help the library system which does not have the resources to start from scratch. If questionnaires are able to cover all areas of possible need there will be a stronger chance of more valid results.

The use of questionnaires enables us to contact all members of staff, and possibly all the users, of an organization. We can hope to obtain views from individuals about how they perceive their training need directly related to the aims and objectives of the system, and the respondents may also volunteer valuable additional information. However, the responses contained within the forms may be as questionable as those on the complaint forms. All data so collected must be double-checked and verified by more personal contact. Workshops can be held, to which representative groups of staff can be invited, and information can be checked.

3.1.9   *Direct observation/self-observation*

An alternative method of identifying training need is the *direct observation technique*. The library trainer or, in some cases a specialized analyst, observes the member of staff at work and determines the training need from what they see. It should be noted that this system does not generally allow much personal interaction between the individual and the needs analyst. It will also be important to use a credible observer who has the trust and confidence of staff. In general industry it would be quite usual for outside consultants to be brought in for this kind of work. The main advantage of this process is that it avoids any difficulty which might be caused by the post-holder's unwillingness or inability to define, or be aware of, their own needs. This type of observation may be useful for routine, understandable work but will not be so effective for the study of jobs that incorporate irregular or very infrequently performed tasks.

If it is simply a question of obtaining job data (e.g. how long a particular sequence of tasks may be taking) then it may be worth considering establishing some kind of *self-logging observation* system where the post-holder will be asked to record details about how they are performing particular tasks. Questionnaires themselves, of course, can be a form of self-logging technique. The member of staff might also be issued with a work diary or checklist for completion. The *problem incident technique* asks the job-holder to write down the most difficult task performed during the past day or week. From an analysis of perceived problem areas it may be possible to identify training need.

3.1.10 | *Interviews*

Interviews of one kind or another are usually an important element of TNA. A common scenario will be for individual one-to-one interviews to follow the circulation and completion of a questionnaire. In this way they are able to act as a useful verification process and may enable the library trainer to develop basic comments appearing among the responses.

All managers will be familiar with the need to acquire good interviewing techniques for a whole variety of purposes. Interviews relating to the identification of training skills will require exactly the same skills.

* Good preparation must take place well before the date of the interview. If a questionnaire or pre-interview form has been used both the interviewer and the interviewee must have had adequate time in which to consider the responses. The post-holder should always be very clear about the purpose of the interview.
* The meeting should take place in an appropriate environment. Staff should be comfortable and at ease, and care should be taken to ensure that there are no interruptions. It may be useful to consider the possibility of taking the member of staff away from his or her place of work.
* The time-scale should be defined: ideally, no longer than two hours with the possibility of further meetings if necessary.
* The interviewer must use competent questioning, listening and response skills in order to encourage the full participation of the interviewee. Care should be taken not to accept opinions, hearsay and subjective observations, automatically.
* When specifically investigating the content of a job, it may be useful to undertake a series of interviews with post-holders on the same level in order to check consistency and accuracy. It will also be wise to interview post-holders from different levels within the structure who may have a relationship with the job. When dealing with a sequence of interviews from different levels within the establishment it will usually be advisable to begin with the most senior member of staff. This has the advantage of establishing reasons and benefits at the highest level first and also tends to give a more general picture of operations before the need to investigate detail.
* A full record of the interview should be agreed and created as soon as possible.

The need for interviews may arise in many different ways. Formal interviews, such as performance management or staff appraisal interviews, may already be taking place within the organization and may prove to be a useful source for identifying training need. In such an interview one is asking the question, 'Is the member of staff performing satisfactorily?', and whatever the answer to this question may be, it is also necessary to ask: 'Will training help in any way?'. The answers to these questions will lead to a consideration of the kind of training which will be most appropriate.

Interviews can take place in a structured or unstructured way. They can be used to deal with a critical incident or may be arranged to collect data. It may sometimes be advisable to set up special TNA interviews to deal with the subject in isolation, but any interview taking place within a library system may generate training needs, and the library trainer should always maintain a close relationship with direct supervisors, who may be involved in regular interviewing, in order to ensure that all relevant information is collected and recorded appropriately.

Having reviewed the sources of information available and selected the most appropriate combination of methods, the library trainer will now be ready to begin the process of identifying training need.

3.2 Corporate needs analysis

In general industry, it has often been found useful to classify corporate training needs into three main groups:

1 Those caused by change
2 Those which are generated by work problems
3 Those which are suggested by personnel statistics

1 Change always seems to be happening and yet people are often not fully prepared to deal with it comprehensively. A quick 'management of change' course is often all that can be achieved. In fact, a training need will arise whenever the methods and procedures of an organization are adjusted in any way. New methods may not only require a new sequence of activities to be learned, they may also demand the acquisition of new skills and the development of new staff attitudes. They may imply a reduction in staffing levels.

A good library trainer will always be planning ahead in order to minimize the effect of change on their organization. Changes may be brought about by many different reasons and each could require a different approach, from the training point of view. The changes most likely to be faced within libraries are as follows:

- *Technological change.* Improvements in machinery and equipment mean that staff using the equipment will need to learn new techniques and acquire new skills. New attitudes will need to be developed, particularly when new machines are being introduced for the first time.
- *Market changes.* As with every other industry, libraries are often placed in the position of having to consider whether or not they are continuing to meet the needs of their users. Expectations change and librarians must be prepared to change with them. Market changes do not always occur quickly. The steady change in the age structure of the population of a town may ultimately have a major effect on the type of services being required from the local public library. This type of change can generally be anticipated.
- *Legislative change.* Laws are regularly being passed which affect our working environment and which may necessitate some related training. The Health and Safety Regulations are a good example of this and staff involved in recruitment interviewing will need to be fully aware of the anti-discrimination laws.
- *Personnel trends and changes.* Changes in age, quality, type and availability of staff in a particular area may also create new training needs.

Requirements for new entrants may change and induction programmes may, therefore, need amending.

2 When it becomes apparent that an organization or individual is working well below an acceptable level of performance it may indicate that staff
have not been sufficiently developed and trained. Sometimes it will be difficult to identify the real problem as many members of staff will be reluctant to admit that they are not fully competent within their post. Again, the
performance interview, if it is conducted in a positive and unthreatening
way, can be very useful in identifying work problems.
Work problems may arise because of:

- Structural problems within the organization
- Health and safety matters
- Lack of training in customer care
- Lack of delegation
- Specific methods and processes being followed
- Quality control

For some problems which may be work orientated, training may be able to
provide only a partial solution.

3 Excessive staff turnover can also indicate a training need within an
organization and it may be useful for the library trainer to assess what
might constitute an acceptable level of turnover. General manpower difficulties may indicate any of the following organizational problems, all of
which can be overcome by training:

- Inadequate induction process
- Poor selection and recruitment practice
- Lack of career development or advice
- Poor salary/reward structure
- Interpersonal conflict
- Poor communication
- Age/experience distribution throughout the organization

3.3 Individual needs analysis

An individual's training needs can be derived from two main sources.
Some will come directly from the corporate needs which have already been
identified. From these it should be possible to determine which members
of staff, or groups of staff, need to be trained now, or at some time in the
future. Corporate analysis can be undertaken by the library trainer or by
members of a senior management or training team but it will always be
important for good communication to take place throughout the whole
organization in order to maintain the commitment of the individual.
Other needs can be identified by comparing the performance achieved
by a member of staff with the performance demands of the job. This
method needs the full involvement of the individuals, who are often in the
best position to be able to identify deficiencies within themselves and will
need to acquire the motivation to change.
TNA must use both methods to achieve comprehensive results and,
therefore, it will be important for the whole process to be a highly partici-

pative one. It will require the full acceptance of the staff who may ultimately be in need of training. Individuals will usually be positively motivated to improve their performance if they are able to feel that there has also been a full recognition of their own personal and development needs.

The initial stages of TNA will identify areas of need which can generally be met by induction or tasks and skills training. However, it will be only by the involvement of the whole library system that development training needs can begin to be addressed. By identifying and clarifying the aims and objectives of our organizations those responsible for TNA may have begun to identify some broad development needs but one must have the involvement of colleagues in order to test and confirm original findings. Managers may also wish to build and develop more personal needs within the plan.

In any system which is operating a performance management or staff appraisal scheme it should be a simple matter to identify individual training need. The minimum process will usually include an annual interview between member of staff and direct supervisor, and training needs arising out of this interview should be fully discussed and recorded. The purpose of such a scheme will be to improve individual performance and to try to relate it to wider issues throughout the organization by the setting of short-term goals and objectives. This all falls neatly within the original definition of identification of need; one can expect that the establishment of training needs will be included. Although most of the information generated during the interview must, of necessity, be restricted to no more than two direct supervisors and the member of staff, there is now provision in most systems for the library trainer to receive copies of the sections of the documentation relating to training. In this way it becomes possible for identified needs to be grouped together, if thought desirable, and finally they may become part of a wider corporate need.

Where performance management schemes do not exist it will be necessary for organizations to devise a process for themselves. Schemes can vary widely as they have often been created locally. In most cases the process will consist of the use of a questionnaire to all or some members of staff, followed by one-to-one interviews. This may be supplemented by workshops and the use of other training activities and sources.

Good preparation will always be important and effective communication will be essential. The best schemes begin with some kind of presentation process, clearly defining the purpose and content of proposed exercises. Full commitment must be obtained and maintained.

Some organizations involve only the individual members of staff themselves while others include the immediate supervisor and colleagues within the identification process. This can be a very sensitive issue and may give rise to concern from individuals. However the investigation is to be conducted, it should be clear that this is intended to be an open, non-threatening exercise. It is helpful for both individual and supervisor to record comments on need and for these to be discussed between them in a constructive way. Ideally, the final list of identified needs should be a jointly agreed submission.

Whatever type of process is chosen, it will be important for it to be absorbed easily within the structure of the organization. An existing performance management scheme has the advantage of being able to facilitate this. It may be more appropriate to introduce TNA in a more individual and specific way in order to ensure full understanding and engagement. TNA can have a considerable impact on an organization, and a specialized programme may be particularly relevant after a period of restructuring and reorganization. It must be remembered, however, that the process has to be continuous to achieve any lasting results. A programme which cannot be sustained may be counter-productive. Some library systems have organized an initial programme with a high profile and have then incorporated TNA within their performance management process. Others have felt strongly that performance management is too closely related to assessment and performance scoring to be fully effective as an identification method. Possibly the most successful schemes are the ones which follow the initial questionnaires with a special TNA interview which then becomes a regular annual interview in its own right. This may be time-consuming but can become an invaluable tool for the collection of training data. Training plans and programmes can be effectively updated on an annual basis.

4 Analysis of training need

Having identified performance objectives and problems within an organization and having agreed which of these can be met by a training solution, the library trainer will be ready to begin to analyse how these needs might be provided for.

The identification of needs process should have produced a comprehensive schedule of particular needs which can be listed and grouped. These will have been determined by either corporate or individual analysis but will all relate either to a particular member of staff or to an identifiable group or groups of staff within the system. Within this earlier process, it might be considered helpful to break down the staff establishment into understandable, generic groups. In preparing your full training plan, this will become critical. However, care must be taken to avoid generalizing too freely. For example, it may be possible to define the posts of 'library assistant' or 'library supervisor', and to relate specific training needs to them. This may take care of the majority of needs but the library trainer must still be aware of the possibility of one particular need being identified which might relate to only one member of the identified group.

The identification process should have provided us with a list of training needs which can be set against our total staff establishment, either grouped generically or listed individually. Depending upon the size and type of library system, one must now begin to define the final format of the training plan before proceeding further (see Chapter 6).

The next task will be to analyse each particular training need in order to determine how best it might be met. It will not be sufficient to say that training is required. The trainer must be able confidently to identify:

- What kind of training?
- Who will deliver it?
- How will it be delivered?
- Where will it be delivered?
- Why will it be delivered?

Examining each need, the following questions must be asked:

- Does this training need apply to one particular group of staff at a particular location?
- Does the need apply to only one person or to a few individuals?
- Does this need apply throughout the whole organization?
- Is this a need which we anticipate (pro-active) or one which has arisen out of current concern about performance (re-active)?
- Does the need involve some kind of specialized knowledge or skill which our staff may find difficult to learn or acquire?
- Is the need relevant only to a particular type of job or is it more global?

- Will the satisfaction of this particular need be cost-effective for the organization as a whole?

By this stage the trainer will have disposed of most of the performance discrepancies which can be solved in other ways. Nevertheless, one must still be alert to the possibility of other alternatives being preferable. In particular, *training needs* and *education needs* should not be confused. Through our research we are likely to encounter many needs which can be met only by education (academic; upgrading; long-term professional need etc.). An education need, though no less important than a training need, must be dealt with separately.

When differentiating between education and training, it may be useful to remember the '*human learning pyramid*' with its large base of 'life experience', on which is laid our 'education', generally given in some kind of formal way. 'Training' appears at the top of the pyramid which is closest to the actual work situation and provides a focus towards the activities of one's post.

The choice of correct method to meet each training need will be critical to the success of the whole TNA process. During the identification process, possibilities will be suggested and tested. There will be many options to consider, including the following:

- External courses
- Internal courses
- On-the-job training
- Observation
- Role-play
- Self-learning
- Secondment
- Workshops
- Demonstrations
- Case studies
- Lectures
- Computer-assisted instruction
- Discussions
- Tests
- Internal programmes
- Open learning
- Shadowing
- Guided reading
- Visits
- Transfers

Many training needs can be fully or partially met by the provision of training aids such as:

- Videos/booklets/manuals/checklists/self-learning units etc.

The production of such aids may be the most cost-effective solution.

The possibilities are almost endless and the library trainer must give careful consideration to each option. It may be a difficult task to persuade colleagues that not all training needs can necessarily justify the setting up of a training course. Similarly, sending staff away to an external course can be a very expensive option which may produce a limited end result. The correct choices will, of course, vary between different organizations, even when we are dealing with the same need. Before taking any final decision, the following matters should be considered:

- *What is the organizational climate?* Is training regarded positively or with suspicion? Are things currently going well and are hopes and standards high? Is the sixth recent restructuring about to take place and is staff morale at an all-time low? Remember that training can always be positively promoted and fully justified in a retrenchment situation.

- *What training resources already exist within the organization?* Is there a local training unit within the system or a larger training department within a containing organization? Are these facilities conveniently available and at what cost? Is a training programme already in operation? Are suitable training venues available? Are they suitably equipped?
- *The specific make-up of the staff* will be important. Age, education, experience and current state of morale may all have a significant bearing on the likely success of the method chosen. What expectations of training exist within the workforce?
- *The structure of the organization* and the exigencies of the service will need to be considered carefully. If a certain group of staff receives training, will a library have to close? If one group of staff, or an individual member of staff, receives training, will this affect others? Are libraries and service points scattered geographically? Will it be difficult to bring together staff of a certain type? The answers to this kind of question will influence whether or not it is possible to centralize training. Will it be necessary to take training to several sites? Will open learning be an option? Can on-the-job training take place without seriously disrupting the service being provided?
- *How long is the method going to take?* Will training be accomplished in half a day or within three months? Will this involve replacement costs?
- *What kind of learning style will be required?* Learning may be divided between *cognitive* and *behavioural* styles. Much of it may be a combination of the two. Routine tasks and activities requiring manual dexterity will fall within the behavioural style and may indicate the need for practical workshops, 'hands-on' testing and the development of experience. Problem-solving, decision-making and analytical work fall completely within the cognitive style and may suggest lectures, demonstrations or some form of role-play. Many activities such as professional work or general trouble-shooting will require an element of both learning styles. Particular training methods will be appropriate for particular learning requirements. It may be very important, for example, for the training to be undertaken within the actual workplace or there may be advantages in removing staff to a neutral learning environment.
- *The complexity of the training required* may tend to influence whether or not it can be provided easily by the organization itself or if expert advice and expertise must be sought. A complex training need might have to be addressed by a variety of methods.
- *The needs of individuals* may or may not be related to the needs of the group. It may seem to be a good idea to take advantage of a training programme in order to bring together staff but this could be an expensive luxury. Training staff for work which may not be immediately relevant to their need can only result in frustration.
- *Is the perceived need a proactive or a reactive one?* The need may have arisen because of a major problem within the organization which needs addressing immediately. In a reactive situation, staff are likely to have the opportunity of using the training they have acquired quickly. On the other hand, a proactive need may have been identified because a new work process is coming into operation next year. It may be counter-productive for training to commence too early. Generally, one should aim to ensure that staff are able to demonstrate their new skills or knowledge in the workplace within one month of the training being undertaken.

- *External factors* may influence the decision. Legal requirements may force managers to review priorities. External funding may be available for particular types of training only. Particular kinds of training provision may be readily available from the Library Association or other agencies.
- *The comparison of cost with ultimate benefit to the organization* should always be one of our most important considerations. Indeed, trainers may have to demonstrate this before any activity can be undertaken. It may be very difficult to establish but it is important to try to do so. For any programme it should be possible to explain:

1 How this will benefit the organization
2 What the economic impact on the organization would be if the training did not take place

One may also wish to consider whether or not cooperation with other local library systems is possible and if this is a training service for which we can make a charge.

- Finally one must revert to the reconsideration of *organizational aims and objectives*. They may affect the choice of method significantly. If a particular type of service is to be discontinued in the near future it may be undesirable to continue to ensure that all new staff are trained to provide it. The library trainer must always be aware of current aims and priorities in order to make sure that the training programmes remain current and relevant.

Careful analysis of training needs within the TNA process is time-consuming and can sometimes be difficult. However, it is essential to identify the correct design for the right purpose. Poor work at this stage may mean that the whole exercise has been pointless.

5 Setting of training objectives

The library trainer should, by now, be fully aware of the objectives of the organization and the more specific performance objectives. It should be a simple matter to translate these into training objectives linked closely to the earlier analysis of training needs.

The work of analysis will have provided useful clues. It may be vital, for example, to be able to meet one objective before moving on to another. Time-scale may indicate a logical sequence of objectives. Different elements of the ultimate training plan can require very different objectives but relationships may have to be maintained.

If the organization did not have any clearly identifiable objectives to begin with, the setting of the training objectives will be all the more important. It is not a stage of the work which can be dealt with in a perfunctory way.

It is becoming more and more common for library organizations to produce and publish individual strategies or business plans relating to their training needs. These can become the framework upon which the full training plan can be based. They should be more constant than the individual training programmes which will be based on them but, like all areas of the training process, they will require regular review and amendment (see Appendix 3).

6 The training plan

Having completed the TNA process and established objectives and priorities, it is necessary to consider whether or not all the information collected could usefully be incorporated into a training plan.

This may be a time-consuming operation but a comprehensive published plan can be a useful aid and support to any training programme. It can help all staff, within a large system, to understand fully how aims and objectives are being reached. Perhaps the most useful plans are those which can be broken down into their constituent elements to be used as working documents. A training plan, however documented and distributed, will include any or all of the following components:

- *Details of the training objectives of the organization.* These may be incorporated into succinct statements of intent relating either to the programme as a whole or to individual parts of it, or may be developed into a detailed strategy explaining:

  - Training philosophy and general principles
  - Training priorities
  - Training implementation and the role of both trainers and trainees

A general statement of aims and objectives might be as follows:

> *'The purpose of the plan is to provide advice and facilities to enable members of staff to acquire the necessary skills and knowledge to perform effectively the duties for which they were employed, and to develop themselves in order to meet the future needs of both the organization and the profession.*
>
> *The organization has stated that its staff are the Service's greatest asset. The Library Service is committed to invest in their training, support and development in order to recruit and retain a high quality of staff.'*

- *The main body of the plan* should list identified training needs clearly set against individuals or levels of staff to be trained, and should specify the agreed method of training and where the responsibility for this training lies. Priorities and time-scale may be defined.

Plans come in many shapes and sizes and there will be as many different views about preferred practice. Presentation will probably reflect the way in which the TNA has been undertaken and this will be useful at the monitoring and evaluation stage. For example, one organization may choose to present its plan divided into the three broad areas of training provision (induction, tasks and skills, and development). There will generally be broad aims and objectives for each area. Within this framework, all groups of staff will be listed showing their own training objectives and the way in which this training will be undertaken. Another type of presentation might arrange all the training needs under defined groups of staff, which has the advantage of enabling individuals to identify complete training objectives from their own point of view.

The plan might be completed by practical examples of training forms and documentation, relevant checklists and full information about the practical aspects of the programme (see Appendix 3).

Some trainees will prefer to be more specific about strategy and objectives rather than going into too much detail about individual programmes and may maintain a parallel, ever-changing series of programmes in accordance with the broad stated priorities in the plan. This must be a local decision and practice will vary according to the training resources available. At the end of the day the most important objective is that a comprehensive TNA exercise has taken place and that training is clearly being provided in accordance with the defined conclusions.

7 Monitoring and evaluation

No management or training cycle would be complete without a brief reference to the continuing importance of the monitoring and evaluation process.

There should be two parts of the assessment procedure. The first will check to see if the training programme has met its particular aim and if behaviour has changed. The second will be concerned with assessing the overall value of the total training programme to the organization.

It is vital that some form of evaluation takes place with reference to all training provision and this can be introduced in many different ways. The results of such evaluation will ultimately become an essential part of future work in TNA and will help to up-date, moderate and redesign our approach to the ever-changing pattern of training need.

8 Preparing for TNA

It is easy to avoid a systematic analysis of training needs by putting forward many of the excuses referred to earlier. The best work in TNA tends to be done when somebody moves to a new position of authority when there will be many reasons for wanting to examine and review demands, performance and priorities. Within library and information work, it is rare to come across continuing examples of good practice spanning many years. Where this does occur it is generally the by-product of some other kind of management process such as the long-term effects of a staff appraisal scheme.

Excuses are easy to find and yet there are few organizations that undertake no training at all. Training which is not linked to true analytical techniques is unlikely to be completely effective and is probably costing time and resources.

Any library trainer can become a 'consultant' within their own system and, with a little experience, should be able to identify key matters of concern. A consultant will then seek to help the members of an organization identify and face up to their problems. Consultation usually involves the following steps:

- Making contact and establishing a 'contract'
- Gathering information and analysing that information
- Planning various alternatives and devising strategies in order to implement these alternatives
- Bringing about change
- Following up on change

This structure can also be said neatly to summarize the TNA process.

The approach will vary according to position within the hierarchy of the organization. More often than not the boss, the users and colleagues will need to be persuaded that what is being done is cost-effective and sensible. It is important to define the client and to ensure that the final contract is drawn up carefully.

Certain questions will need to be asked and answered at the start:

- What is the relationship with the clients within the organization (i.e. boss; users; colleagues) and how are they likely to relate to us?
- How is the process going to begin?
- What do our clients expect of us?
- To what extent are they dependent on us?
- Do any continuing links or relationships need to be maintained during the work?
- How near will you be to the decision-making process of the organization?
- Will you have full access to all relevant information sources and staff?

- Does the client have a history of commitment to change?
- Does the client understand the basic principles of TNA?

It will be useful to establish a working group in order to ensure that all aspects of the exercise are fully covered. Perhaps a training working party already exists within the organization which could give valuable help and support. At the end of the day one is looking for the full commitment and involvement of the organization and it may be necessary to spend some preliminary time ensuring that this will be forthcoming.

You will need to make sure that you have answered the following questions:

- How is activity going to commence?
- Who is the decision-maker who is going to make it happen?
- What will be the exact role of yourself and your team?
- What is the time-scale of the operation?
- How will you know when the exercise is completed?

It will be very important for any consultant to relate well to all the clients and, in most of our cases, this is likely to mean all the staff and, possibly, most of the users as well. One must build up a relationship of trust and ensure that good communication takes place at all times.

A formal or informal contract needs to be established with the clients before any real work is undertaken. One must be clear about the client's expectations and will need to share understanding of the TNA process with clients.

Look for and be prepared to deal with concern from client groups. Staff will always be apprehensive about any kind of process which seeks to examine performance, and regular reassurance may be necessary. Resist any temptation to become dictatorial or autocratic. The best type of TNA can only take place in an atmosphere of good corporate management. Involve all of the key people within the organization in the exercise as much as possible. Always be prepared to discuss concerns and consider changes of direction.

Finally, the whole process will need to be explained fully to all the participants, together with details about what it is hoped to achieve and what benefits the organization and individual members of staff may reasonably expect. If questionnaires are to be used, then it will be necessary to introduce them carefully. If interviews are being set up, preliminary training may well be desirable and reassuring.

Any library system which has undertaken a comprehensive programme of TNA can be confident that it will be able to use its resources wisely to provide the best training possible. Most librarians are aware that good training will result in an improved image for the organization and a better service for the users. The staff should become more competent and motivated and work can be related directly to positive cost savings. Good TNA is the only reliable way of ensuring that the right amount of the right sort of training is provided to the right sort of people at exactly the right time.

⑨ Summary

This guide has provided a broad introduction to training needs analysis. After establishing basic terms, the place of TNA within the wider training framework has been examined and defined. In particular, the close relationship of TNA to good cost-effective management has been noted.

The complete process of TNA has been explored, beginning with the necessity to identify and establish clear aims and objectives for the organization. A constant awareness for possible problems in performance leads naturally to identified concerns, most of which can be dealt with by the provision of training. The identification and analysis of these training needs will combine to assist in the setting of comprehensive training objectives and these, in turn, will help to formulate the final training plan for the organization.

The processes of determining and analysing training needs have been examined in some detail. Possible training aids and sources have been suggested and evaluated, and the relationship between corporate and individual needs analysis has been reviewed.

The TNA cycle has been followed from the initial identification of aims and objectives to the continuous need for monitoring and evaluation of all training, thus providing the constant probability of amendment and fine-tuning.

Finally, consideration has been given to the practical preparation for TNA within the organization. A systematic and comprehensive approach to training will always be cost-effective eventually and success can be demonstrated easily. Unfortunately, many are deterred from an analytical approach by mistaken fears and concerns. The library trainer who perseveres through the time-consuming earlier stages of TNA can ultimately be confident of success.

The final chapter of the Guide provides some brief information about sources which may be helpful when undertaking a TNA exercise. This is followed by some examples of good practice from within the profession.

10 Select bibliography and useful contacts

10.1 Select bibliography

Applegarth, Michael, *How to take a training audit*, London, Kogan Page, 1990.

Conyers, Angela, 'Staff training and effectiveness', in *Personnel management in polytechnic libraries*, ed. Don Revill, Aldershot, Gower, 1987.

Jones, Noragh and Jordan, Peter J., *Staff management in library and information work*, 2nd edn, Aldershot, Gower, 1987. (3rd edn in preparation: approximate publication date: summer 1994).

Parry, Julie, 'Training needs assessment (TNA): its place in an effective training programme', *Learning resources journal*, Oct. 1991, 62–6 (illus.).

Peterson, Robyn, *Training needs analysis in the workplace*, London, Kogan Page, 1992.

Public Library Development Incentive Scheme (PLDIS), *Co-operative training, open learning and public library staffs*, prepared by the Northern Training Group and the Scottish Council for Educational Technology, Glasgow, Nov. 1992.

Turrell, M., *Training analysis. A guide to recognising training needs*, Plymouth, Macdonald and Evans, 1980.

10.2 Useful contacts

A selection of organizations which publish material, train or provide a consultancy service.

BACIE
The British Association for Commercial and Industrial Education offers courses and produces publications including a journal on training methods. Write to: BACIE, 16 Park Crescent, Regent's Park, London W1N 4AP. Telephone: 071-636 5351. (After 16 April 1995, 0171-636 5351).

The Institute of Management
For more information write to:
Management House, Cottingham Road, Corby, Northamptonshire NN17 1TT. Telephone: 0536 204222. (After 16 April 1995, 01536 204222).

Industrial Society
For more information write to:
Quadrant Court, 29 Calthorpe Road, Edgbaston, Birmingham B15 1TH. Telephone: 021-454 6769. (After 16 April 1995, 0121-454 6769).

LGMB (Local Government Management Board)
Among the responsibilities of the Local Government Training Board is supporting the training of people with management responsibility in local

authorities. The LGMB publishes several manuals containing practical materials for management training. For further information write to:
Local Government Training Board, 4th Floor, Arndale House, Arndale Centre, Luton LU1 2TS. Telephone: 0582 451166. (After 16 April 1995, 01582 451166).

Continuing Education Unit, Bristol University

The Continuing Education Unit is managed by the Department of Management at Bristol University and produces a wide range of management training resources in the form of exercises, papers, overhead projector transparencies and summary sheets. These resources provide material for training course input on most management topics. Visitors are welcome and may browse among the materials and purchase collections and individual items. Contact:
The Manager, Continuing Education Unit, Room 3B5, Bristol University, Coldharbour Lane, Frenchay, Bristol BS16 1QY. Telephone: 0272 656261 ext. 278. (After 16 April 1995, 0117 965 6261).

Open University

The Open University provides a number of distance learning courses and publishes related materials covering the whole field of educational management and training. For information on courses write to:
Admissions Office, The Open University, PO Box 48, Walton Hall, Milton Keynes MK7 6AB. Telephone: 0908 274066. (After 16 april 1995, 01908 274066).

Many materials are readily available in libraries. For information on materials write to:
Open University Educational Enterprises Limited, 12 Cofferidge Close, Stony Stratford, Milton Keynes MK11 1BY. Telephone: 0908 261662. (After 16 April 1995, 01908 261662).

Appendix 1
Cooperative training, open learning and public library staff

This project was initiated by the Northern Training Group with funding from the Public Library Development Incentive Scheme and in collaboration with Information North, local Training and Enterprise Councils, the Local Government Management Board and the Scottish Council for Educational Technology. The first phase, which has already taken place, set out to establish priority training needs across the ten authorities, for which adequate training material was not available, and which could justify investment in open learning materials. The second phase will concentrate on the development and production of these materials and supporting systems.

This detailed investigation, which demonstrates some of the many advantages of cooperative training, identified key training needs which were common to all the constituent authorities. It was discovered that satisfactory provision for some of these needs is not readily available (either because it does not exist or is not accessible, or because of quality or cost considerations) and that some of the gaps in provision can be met by open learning as the preferred method.

The Interim Report on the first phase of this project, prepared by the Northern Training Group and SCET, was published in November 1992 and copies are available from Information North.

Appendix 2
Examples of TNA forms

Example 1   The Guildhall Library. Corporation of London.
Example of form and covering letters to all staff and section heads.

Example 2   East Sussex Library Service.
Training Needs Assessment Scheme.
Notes of Guidance for Interviewees and Counsellors.

Example 3 Suffolk County Council: Arts and Libraries
Training Needs Analysis Programme.
Aims and Objectives: covering letter and two sample questionnaire
sheets.

Example 1

Libraries and Art Galleries Department

Training Needs Analysis

Name _____

Post _____

Section _____

The following training needs have been identified:-

1.   Urgent/Necessary/Desirable

2.   Urgent/Necessary/Desirable

3.   Urgent/Necessary/Desirable

4.   Urgent/Necessary/Desirable

Comments:-

Signed _____Post Holder

_____Interviewing Officer

_____Section Head (if not interviewer)

Date _____

Example 1 continued

LIBRARIES AND ART GALLERIES DEPARTMENT

TRAINING NEEDS ANALYSIS

To Section Heads

As part of the Department's commitment to Training Needs Analysis, you are expected to arrange for an individual discussion annually with each member of your staff on likely training needs. It is at your discretion how you organise this process within your Section. You may wish to conduct all the discussion sessions yourself or you may prefer to delegate some of them.

You should discuss any training needs which have been identified by yourself and senior colleagues, and staff should be encouraged to put forward their own suggestions for training which will benefit the Department. However, all requests must be realistic as it is vital to ensure that staff can be released to undertake any training which may be agreed.

Following the discussion, in order to avoid any misunderstandings, a Training Needs Analysis form should be completed and signed by the parties involved. All forms should be countersigned by the Section Head whether or not he/she conducted the interview. A copy should be retained by the member of staff concerned and a copy forwarded to the Planning and Resources Librarian. Where no training needs are identified, nil returns are required.

Your own training needs will be explored in a discussion with the Deputy Director.

The deadline for the return of Training Needs Analysis forms this year will be 31st October 1990.

The training budget for 1990/91 has already been finalised, but the information provided will be used when allocating that budget and in bidding for resources in 1991/2.

A brief description of the Training Needs Analysis scheme, circulated to all staff, is attached. If you have any queries please contact the Planning and Resources Librarian.

Example 1 continued

LIBRARIES AND ART GALLERIES DEPARTMENT

TRAINING NEEDS ANALYSIS

To all staff

Some time in the next few months you will be invited to discuss your training needs for the coming year with your Section Head or another senior member of your Section's staff. Please study the attached description of the Training Needs Analysis Scheme and consider carefully what your training needs are.

You will be encouraged to put forward your own ideas during the discussion. We will be looking for suggestions that will benefit the Department as a whole. Please be realistic as well as imaginative!

The training budget for 1990/91 has already been finalised, but the information provided will be used when allocating that budget and in bidding for resources in 1991/2. The deadline for the return of the Training Needs Analysis forms this year will be 31st October 1990.

If you have any queries on the scheme, please speak, in the first instance to your Section Head.

Example 2

EAST SUSSEX COUNTY LIBRARY SERVICE

TRAINING NEEDS ASSESSMENT SCHEME

Notes of guidance for Counsellors

Each year the East Sussex County Library Service undertakes a Training Needs Assessment [TNA] involving all staff up to middle management level. The results of the process enables the organisation to plan its training programme for the next financial year. More importantly, the TNA process gives every member of staff concerned the opportunity to discuss their own training and development with their manager or supervisor on a one-to-one basis.

The counselling interviews for the current round of TNA will soon be underway. The following notes are intended to outline the scheme for those staff new to conducting counselling interviews, or, to act as a reminder for those who have experienced it before.

A. STAGES IN THE TNA PROCESS

1. Arrange a date for the counselling session with the job holder. This should be done well in advance, to allow the job holder time to complete Section 1 of the TNA form and return it to you.

2. Complete Section 2 of the form and return form to the job holder.

3. At the end of the counselling interview, complete Sections 3 and 4. The form should then be signed by you both as an agreed record.

4. Take two photocopies of the completed form, one for yourself and one for the job holder. Send the original form to the Training Officer at Library Headquarters for collation and analysis.

5. Once all forms have been received and the departmental training needs assessed, each interviewee will receive a letter outlining the action being taken on his/her training and development recommendations. You will receive a copy of that letter.

The contents of all completed forms will remain confidential and be used only for the purposes of the Training Needs Assessment Scheme.

Example 2 continued

B. THE COUNSELLING INTERVIEW

Each counsellor will develop his or her way of handling the session but the following should be used as basic guidelines.

1. Ensure that the place where the interview will be held is private and free from interruptions. Aim for a relaxed, informal atmosphere.

2. Study the interviewee's job description before the interview. Have a checklist of points to cover, and all necessary facts.

3. Explain the purpose of the discussion; ensure that both parties have similar objectives.

4. Concentrate on achievements and results. Encourage the interviewee to acknowledge successes and identify any limitations or failures. Together, work out ways of redressing the negative points.

5. The interviewee should have an equal part in the discussion; encourage the interviewee to talk about the job and the circumstances in which it is undertaken. Listen to what the interviewee is saying; use exploratory questions to help the interviewee to initiate any areas of concern.

6. Do not compare the interviewee's work with others. It has no validity for the individual, his/her work performance is unique.

7. The discussion must be forward looking; an opportunity to solve problems. It should be directed towards further action in areas of mutual concern.

8. Do not make promises you (or the organisation) will be unable to fulfil, e.g. because of the cost, or time involved.

9. Summarise at intervals throughout the discussion. At the end, both parties should be quite clear about what has been agreed and the main point recorded. If there is disagreement over any aspect of the discussion which cannot be resolved, this should be noted for consideration at a higher level.

C. TRAINING AND DEVELOPMENT METHODS

Section 4 of the Training Needs Assessment form is for training and development recommendations. It is important when considering these that the whole range of methods which could be used are considered. The following list may act as a guide when considering priorities and methods.

1. Study for formal qualifications such as LIAC, BTEC, etc.
    Could be studied at a local college, or by distance learning.

2. External courses. These range from a few hours to several months. Usually run by Professional Associations, Consultants, Universities, Polytechnics, etc. They can cover general or specific topics at all levels of knowledge and skills. Material may not all be relevant and these can be expensive, but participants have the advantage of working with employees from other organisations.

Example 2 continued

3.   In-service courses. There are a wide variety of these, offered in regular programmes from the County Personnel, County Management Services, and Occupational Health Departments, as well as events organised within the County Library. Courses can be specifically designed to meet the training needs of a particular group of staff.

4.   Counselling and coaching.

5.   On-the-job training.

6.   Planned work experience/job rotation.

7.   Membership of working parties.

8.   Visits. (Training objectives should be explicit.)

9.   Individual/group projects. To provide the opportunity to learn from new work in which the trainee has limited experience.

10.   Attachment or secondment. Could be within the department or to an outside organisation. This is often only practical on a reciprocal basis, or as cover for long term leave.

11.   Guided reading.

D.   PRIORITIES

The priorities for the allocation of the finance available for training are as follows:-

1   Essential of Statutory Training
    The training which must be carried out to ensure that employees are able to fulfil the requirements of the job.

2.   Organisational Training
    This will reflect county or departmental policy.

3.   Education
    Some staff may need to study for a formal qualification essential to their job, or one which may be desirable to enable them to pursue a career at a higher level within the department or elsewhere in Local Government.

4.   Optional Training
    Any other areas of training, which are desirable but not essential.

N.B. Although the TNA process gives every member of staff the opportunity to discuss their training needs once a year, the process should not end there. Training needs may change through the year and your staff should be given every opportunity to continue the discussion of those needs as the occasion arises.

Example 2 continued

EAST SUSSEX COUNTY LIBRARY
TRAINING NEEDS ASSESSMENT SCHEME

Notes of guidance for Interviewees

Each year the East Sussex County Library Service undertakes a Training Needs Assessment [TNA] involving all of its staff. The results of the process enables the organisation to plan its training programme for the next financial year. More importantly, the TNA process gives every member of staff concerned the opportunity to discuss their own training and development with their manager or supervisor on a one-to-one basis.

The counselling interviews for the current round of TNA will soon be underway. The following notes are intended to outline the scheme for those staff new to the scheme, or, to act as a reminder for those who have experienced it before.

A   BEFORE THE INTERVIEW

1.   Your manager, or supervisor, will arrange an interview date with you and give you a copy of the TNA form. You will complete Section 1 of the form and return it to your manager, or supervisor, at least one week before the interview date. This will give your manager, or supervisor, time to complete Section 2.

2.   Before you complete Section 1, give some thought to the job you are undertaking. You should have a copy of your job description, if not ask your manager, or supervisor, for a copy. Consider the following questions:-

      – which of the tasks interest you most – why?
      – which of the tasks interest you least – why?
      – are there any areas of the job where you feel you could improve
         your performance, what would help you achieve this?
      – is there any aspect of your job that you do not find satisfactory?
         Why?
      – in your opinion, what are the qualities you bring to your job? –
         think of examples, what are the difficulties? – think of examples
      – have you had any planned work experience or attended any
         training event since your last TNA interview? Did it satisfy your
         original need? if not, why not and what now needs to be done?
      – have you trained or developed others or could you help with
         training and developing others?
      – in an ideal world, how would you see your career in the library
         service progressing? What would help you achieve your ambitions
         in this respect?

Check the results of your last TNA, if applicable. Are there any recommendations still outstanding? Are they still relevant to your job?

3.   When your manager, or supervisor, has completed Section 2, it will be returned to you for you to read the comments before the counselling session.

Example 2 continued

4.	Take your TNA form and job description to your interview, together with any list of points you need to talk about and any information on specific training courses/events that you are particularly interested in.

B	THE COUNSELLING INTERVIEW

This is probably the one time in the year when you have your manager's, or supervisor's undivided attention in discussing your job and your training and development needs. Ensure that the time is well used.

1	Make sure that you understand the purpose of the interview.

2	Keep an open mind, do not decide the outcome of the interview in advance.

3	Relate comments to your work.

4	Be prepared to talk openly and honestly and give your point of view. This will help you to:
(i) identify areas of development in your job
(ii) identify any problem areas
(iii) agree a plan of action.

5	Listen to your manager's, or supervisor's point of view.

6	Don't be aggressive, defensive or over-sensitive to criticism.

7	It is important to be able to recognise achievement.

8	It is equally important to recognise any lack of success, to identify the reasons for it, what help is available to you and to make plans to overcome it.

9	Make sure that objectives are clearly stated, quantifiable and achievable.

Your manager, or supervisor, will summarise the points discussed at intervals throughout the session. On its conclusion you will both agree to the written summary recorded in Section 3 of the TNA form. Any recommendations for training will then be listed, in priority order, in Section 4, together with the objectives your have agreed.

You will both then sign the form, which will be copied twice; one for you and one for your manager, or supervisor. The original will be forwarded to the Training Officer at Headquarters.

The recommendations for training resulting from all the Training Needs Assesment Interviews held will then be collated and analysed, and a Departmental Training Plan for the coming year produced. You will then receive a letter outlining the action being taken on your personal training recommendations.

The contents of all completed forms will remain confidential and be used only for the purposes of the Training Needs Assessment Scheme.

Example 3

2

TRAINING NEEDS

SKILLS/KNOWLEDGE NEEDS ASSESSMENT QUESTIONNAIRE

Attached is the training needs questionnaire related to your current job description. Any information given in this questionnaire will be treated confidentially.

Please complete the following questions and return to Rose Helm at:

> Arts and Libraries Headquarters
> St Andrew House
> County Hall
> Ipswich IP4 2JS

by 12 February 1993.

Please indicate your service point Area:	Bury St Edmunds	[ ]
	Ipswich	[ ]
	Lowestoft	[ ]

| Do you work: | Full-time? | [ ] |
| | Part-time? | [ ] |

Please indicate the group to which your service point belongs:	Group A	[ ]
	Group B	[ ]
	Group C	[ ]
	Group D	[ ]
	Group E	[ ]
	Group F	[ ]

Now please answer the questions detailed overleaf.

Example 3 continued

1

TRAINING NEEDS ANALYSIS

SKILLS/KNOWLEDGE NEEDS ASSESSMENT QUESTIONNAIRE

Please find attached a training needs questionnaire which corresponds to your current job description.

Please complete the questionnaire as instructed; it is lengthy but will help us to identify any specific areas in which there are potential training needs. If you are not absolutely sure of an answer to any question please select the most appropriate answer given as an option. It is important that the information you give us is as accurate as possible if we are to produce a valuable training needs analysis for the department.

We do not require you to give your name; however, should you wish to give it, please note that all the information resulting from this questionnaire will be treated confidentially.

AIMS AND OBJECTIVES

----

1. To determine the overall skills and knowledge of library assistants, enquiry officers and library managers in our Department.

2. To assist the Service Manager (Professional Resources) and the Professional Resources Assistant to determine the current training needs of library assistants, enquiry officers and library managers in our Department.

3. To assist the Service Manager (Professional Resources) and the Professional Resources Assistant in prioritising training needs as identified by the needs assessment.

4. To assist the Service Manager (Professional Resources) and the Professional Resources Assistant in assessing the most effective methods of meeting the needs identified by the assessment.

Example 3 continued

2

SKILLS/KNOWLEDGE NEEDS ASSESSMENT QUESTIONNAIRE

LIBRARY ASSISTANT

SYSTEM SKILLS

1a. Please answer all questions by circling the relevant response:

- as a routine, would you ask a customer to verbally confirm their details when calling up their record without their SCILScard?   YES/NO/NOT SURE/NOT APPLICABLE

- are you confident about finding an item by author/title to satisfy a general enquiry?
YES/NO/NOT SURE/NOT APPLICABLE

- do you know how to deal with a returned item which has not been issued?
YES/NO/NOT SURE/NOT APPLICABLE

- do you know how to register a playgroup?   YES/NO/NOT SURE/NOT APPLICABLE

- as a routine, do you ask the customer any questions when renewing items using the BLK command?   YES/NO/NOT SURE/NOT APPLICABLE

1b. Now please read the following statement:

'Have the ability/knowledge to deal with basic functions and satisfy general enquiries in the Circulation system.'

Please rate your proficiency in this area	Please rate the importance of this area to your job
1 2 3 4 5 6 very not at all	1 2 3 4 5 6 very not at all

2a. Please answer all questions by circling the relevant response:

- do you know how to deal with stock from other service points when operating in back-up?   YES/NO/NOT SURE/NOT APPLICABLE

- do you know how to calculate overdue charges when operating in back-up?
YES/NO/NOT SURE/NOT APPLICABLE

- do you know how to renew items when operating in back-up?
YES/NO/NOT SURE/NOT APPLICABLE

2b. Now please read the following statement:

'Have the ability to use the Circulation back-up system.'

Please rate your proficiency in this area	Please rate the importance of this area to your job
1 2 3 4 5 6 very not at all	1 2 3 4 5 6 very not at all

Example 3 continued

3

SKILLS/KNOWLEDGE NEEDS ASSESSMENT QUESTIONNAIRE

LIBRARY MANAGER

SYSTEM/TECHNICAL SKILLS

Circulation

1a.   Please answer all questions by circling the appropriate response:

- is it good practice to renew STS items using the BLK command?

    YES/NO/NOT SURE/NOT APPLICABLE

- do you always ensure that staff are carefully instructed before allowing them to carry out "system " jobs (e.g. work experience staff, YT personnel)?

    YES/NO/NOT SURE/NOT APPLICABLE

- do you ensure that tasks such as dealing with "in transit" items, with "hold" messages and with returned notices are dealt with on a regular basis?

    YES/NO/NOT SURE/NOT APPLICABLE

- do you have a clear understanding as to what would be considered valid proof of identity when registering a borrower?   YES/NO/NOT SURE/NOT APPLICABLE

- do you fully understand how to use the general commands in the Circulation system, especially with regard to searching the catalogue?

    YES/NO/NOT SURE/NOT APPLICABLE

- does the type of "hold", i.e. Copy, Area, System, take precedence over another, assuming it is not flagged as priority?

    YES/NO/NOT SURE/NOT APPLICABLE

1b.   Now please read the following statement:

"Have an in-depth knowledge of the Circulation system, understanding what is regarded as good practice, and am especially conversant with the catalogue and able to use it to its full potential."

Please rate your proficiency
in this area

1   2   3   4   5   6
very   not at all

Please rate the importance
of this area to your job

1   2   3   4   5   6
very   not at all

Back-Up

2a.   Please answer all questions by circling the appropriate response:

- do you feel confident in setting-up the parameters on your back-up Micro?

    YES/NO/NOT SURE/NOT APPLICABLE

- do you know how to switch to soft back-up?   YES/NO/NOT SURE/NOT APPLICABLE

- do you know the difference between micro back-up and soft back-up?

    YES/NO/NOT SURE/NOT APPLICABLE

- do you know how to download transactions and deal with error messages after returning to Circulation?   YES/NO/NOT SURE/NOT APPLICABLE

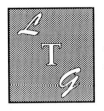

Appendix 3
Examples of training objectives and plans

Example 1   London Borough of Hounslow.
   Training Strategy for Cultural Services.

Example 2   Northamptonshire County Council: Education and Libraries.
   Training Philosophy.
   (The full published Training and Development Strategy of the Libraries
   and Information Service is available for purchase. Information may be
   obtained on 0604 20262 ext. 405.)

Example 3 Hertfordshire Libraries, Arts and Information.
   Introducton and sample page from the current Training Business Plan.

Example 4 Cambridgeshire Libraries and Information Service.
   Sample pages from the Departmental Training Plan.

Example 1

LONDON BOROUGH OF HOUNSLOW
TRAINING STRATEGY FOR CULTURAL SERVICES.

INTRODUCTION

A Leisure Services Training Strategy was produced in 1991 by the Personnel Section of Leisure Services outlining the strategy for the department. This set out the aims and objectives, needs, resources, budgets, training methods, and gave recommendations.

The Cultural Services Training Strategy, covering Libraries, Bib services, Arts team, PRT, Museums and Halls, has kept within these guidelines and seeks to specify the particular needs of the division, address those issues, and come up with a way of answering those needs.

AIMS AND OBJECTIVES

The aim of the Training Strategy is to advance the Service delivery, and to achieve improved performance from staff at all level The objectives are:
* to enable staff to deliver relevant services;
* to enable staff to manage a changing environment;
* to provide staff with relevant skills to enable them to perform at a level that is beneficial to the department;
* to assist staff in attaining greater knowledge of equalities issues and their relevance to service provision;
* to enable staff to have access to training provision;
* to target training in line with equal opportunity objectives;
* to establish a monitoring system to ensure training objectives

All training programmes will be delivered in the context of departmental aims and will be supportive of corporate aims especially equal opportunities objectives in relation to race, sex, disability and older people.

RESOURCES

These will consist in order of usage of:
Training Budget
In-house skills
Central Training
Leisure Services Training
External consultants

APPLICATION OF RESOURCES

These resouces will be used as effectively and economically as possible by the initial use of in-house skills and internally devised courses. Where this is not possible, Central Training and outside skills will be used to tailor internal courses. If this is impractical, then external courses and trainers will be bought into, but only where it matches needs, and knowledge cannot be acquired by the other methods.

This is all in the context of prioritised training needs, and corporate prerequisites, rather than ad-hoc decisions made in isolation by individuals without reference to corporate strategies.

1

Example 1 continued

STRATEGY

1. Discuss with team leaders:
   * immediate training needs they have discovered, and ways to fill them.
   * skills gaps.
   * longterm training priorities.
   * training their team can offer to other teams.

2. Conduct a Training Needs Analysis by:
   * interviewing all staff
   * writing a report on findings and using this to identify resources within the division and to plan further training.

3. Prepare with team leaders a development plan for each category of staff and ensure its implementation. This to include PDRs.

4. Set up regular meeting with managers to discuss their responsibilities for training, to ensure common aims.

5. Set up a records system to record individual staff members' attendance at training sessions, planned attendances, and training needs.

6. Set up effective monitoring procedures to team leaders specifications and divisional needs.

7. Ensure that adequate resources are made available in the way of training personnel, staff time to participate, equipment, facilities and finance.

8. Ensure that staff are given time to attend courses they need, by seeking to specify a percentage of divisional time to be spent on training, and monitoring this.

9. Carry forward this strategy with support of CSMT.

JOY HARRISON
TRAINING AND DEVELOPMENT OFFICER CULTURAL SERVICES.
JANUARY 1993

2

Example 2

TRAINING PHILOSOPHY

- Northamptonshire County Council's strategic objectives involve enabling staff to reach their full potential and thereby assist the council in the effective and efficient delivery of services of the highest standard to the people of Northamptonshire. Training is vital for both the organisation and the individual to adapt and respond to changes and to meet service objectives.

- Northamptonshire Libraries and Information Service aims to promote a Training Strategy which ensures access to a wide variety of effective training and development opportunities for all staff and which will underpin the following styles and values endorsed by the Audit Commission:
  - understanding the customers
  - responding to the electorate
  - setting and pursuing consistent achievable objectives
  - assignment of clear management responsibilities
  - training and motivation of staff
  - communicating effectively
  - adapting to change

- Training and development should be a partnership between staff, managers and the organisational training function. All staff are encouraged to take responsibility within this partnership for their own training and development; with a view to achieving job effectiveness and satisfaction.

- This clear focus for training and development has enabled concise objectives to be formulated, which are clearly achievable and easily monitored.

  1. to provide staff at all levels with the skills and competencies to contribute to an effective and efficient library and information service;

  2. to identify and develop new skills and competencies to ensure that Northamptonshire Libraries and Information Service continues to provide a high quality service;

  3. to provide staff with the opportunity for personal and professional development for the benefit of themselves and the service;

  4. to monitor the training and development programme to ensure that it meets the needs of the service and its staff.

2

Example 3

Introduction

The Training Strategy for 1992/93 outlines a training philosophy, the short and long term commitments, and where the responsibility for training lies - the role of individuals, line managers and the Training Office.

This is the business plan for the Training Office. The overall aim of the section is:

- to provide a comprehensive training service and resource focused on achieving the corporate and regional business plans and the provision of the best possible public service at all times
- to coordinate a county approach to training in HLAI to provide staff with skills for an effective, innovative and evaluative approach to service delivery.

The objectives detailed in this business plan are to:

i. identify organisational training and development needs, present and future, to support the achievement of business objectives and promote an innovative approach to the service

ii. Coordinate internal provision of training to meet identified needs by bringing together or working with relevant members of staff to design and/or deliver training programmes.

iii. Promote external training events and liaise with external training organisations for the purpose of staff attending events, and using outside expertise as appropriate and feasible within resources.

iv. Monitor and evaluate the benefit of training within the organisation as a whole and for particular groups of staff (on functional/specialist basis) and hence for the organisation.

v. Manage the training budget in order to maximise the benefit from present limited resources and to make projections for future needs.

vi. Provide support for training to Regions, CLs, SLAs, TLs etc. in terms of advice, resources, trainer input.

2

| Example 3 | continued

Objective I: Identify organisational training and development needs, present and future, to support achievement of business objectives and promote an innovative approach to the service.

Action	How done	Who does it	Timescale	Measure	Lead
*Consult with and take direction from the Director and senior management to ensure that training meets future, as well as present, organisational needs	At Forum meetings Regular contact with Director Feedback from COG, Chief Executive etc.	Sue Jenny	Ongoing		Sue
*Consult Regional Management Teams about training needs for coming year	Attend RMT meetings annually	Jenny	By March 1993	Dates set, attendance and feedback	Jenny
*Carry out annual sample needs analysis survey	Survey questionnaire to sample one region	Jenny	By March 1994	Results compiled for input into training plan	Jenny
*Compile suggestions and requests for training from Performance Management and Staff Development interviews	Feedback from ADs, RLs to training office	ADs, RLs and T.O. (Sheila)	ongoing	Results/list for input into training plan	Sue Sheila
*Review and update internal course validation sheet to reflect changes in training provision/style	Ask for comments from staff. Compare with other organisations' forms	Jenny TSG	March 93	new form in use	Jenny
*Encourage and seek out continual feedback from regions about training needs	Informally, attending meetings, Through TSG	Sue, Jenny, Sheila, Meg, TSG	ongoing	record of meetings attended#	

4

Example 3 continued

Objective III: Promote external training events and liaise with external training organisations for the purpose of staff attending events, and using outside expertise as appropriate and feasible within resources

Action	How done	Who does it	Timescale	Measure	Lead
*Encourage staff to identify external courses appropriate for staff to meet business objectives of organisation and own performance contract	In Training Section from promotional leaflets etc By recommendation from staff, regions Checking with staff and managers how relevant training course is to performance objectives.	RLs, CLs, TLs, Sue Jenny	ongoing	Training needs met, course evaluation by those attending, enhancing ability to perform etc.	Jenny
*Advertise courses in Training Bulletin when necessary i.e. when there is competition for limited number of places	Details of courses, aims and objectives in bulletin	Sheila/Meg	approx every 2 months	response to bulletin	Jenny
*Book places and ensure details are communicated to candidates	via Training office	Meg	aim to provide candidate with joining instructions, evaluation form etc. at least 2 weeks before course	successful attendance	Meg

11

Example 4

1. INDUCTION TRAINING

Induction Training refers to the arrangements made by or on behalf of the Management of the Department to familiarise the new employee with the working organisation, welfare and safety matters, general conditions of employment and the work of the section in which he/she is to be employed. It will vary according to level of entry, type of post and the previous experience of the new employee.

Objectives, Methods and Responsibility

The following objectives have been identified with reference to Induction Training:-
Note: Applicable to all examples.

1. 'Training Officer' refers either to the Training Manager, the Library Manager, the Training Officers or to other staff known by them to be effective.

2. These need not be individual activities for each objective as they are inter-related.

	Objectives	Method	Staff Responsible

A) Library Assistants
Senior Library
  Assistants
Library Supervisors
Clerical (Admin)
Drivers
Assistant
  Librarians
	a) To provide the understanding and ability to interpret the library's objectives.	Talks. Role-play.
		Case studies.
		On the spot discussions of situations.
		Observation.
		Internal course.
			Training Officer.
			Immediate
			  Supervisor

Operation
  Managers
Librarians
Principal/Senior
  Librarians
Specialist
  Librarians
Management
Volunteers/
  Shelvers
	b) To give a knowledge of total resources.	Video.
		Visits.
		Transfers.
		Exercises and case studies.
		Observation.
		On the spot discussions of situations.
		Staff meetings.
		Discussions with staff.
			Training Officer
			Departmental
			  Staff
			Immediate
			  Supervisor

	c) To give a knowledge of conditions of service and local facilities, etc.	Talks. Literature. Observation.	Immediate Supervisor
	d) To give a knowledge of training and promotion prospects.	Talks. Literature.	Training Officer Immediate Supervisor
	e) To give a knowledge of the Local Authority and the library's relation to it.	Talks. Internal Course. Video	Training Officer Central Training Officer

-2-

Example 4 continued

	f) To establish the place of the newcomers job in the organisation and its relationship with others.	Talks. Video. Observation. Discussions of situations with staff.	Training Officer Immediate Supervisors

B) <u>Manual</u> (excluding Drivers) As above omitting (b)

2. <u>TASKS AND SKILLS</u>

Tasks and Skills Training refers to arrangements made by or on behalf of the Management of the Department to support and develop an employee within the limits of their current accountabilities. It's main purpose is to enable staff to undertake their present responsibilities effectively and well.

<u>Objectives, Methods and Responsibility</u>

The following objectives have been identified with reference to Tasks and Skills Training:-

		Objectives	Method	Staff Responsible
A)	Library Assistants Drivers Volunteers/ Shelvers	a) To provide an understanding of the needs of the user.	Role play. Case studies. 'Communication games'. Attitude tests. Observation. Discussion with users inside and outside the library. Internal course.	Training Officer Immediate Supervisor
		b) To provide a knowledge of routines associated with the post.	Demonstration. Role play. Video. Observation. On the spot discussion.	Training Officer Immediate Supervisor
		c) To help to communicate with and receive users effectively.	Role play. Video. Observation. On the spot discussion. Internal course.	Training Officer Immediate Supervisor
		d) To help to deal with anti-social behaviour/emergencies and current legislation.	Written instruction. Case studies. Role play. Observation. On the spot discussion. Internal course.	Training Officer Police, etc. Immediate Supervisor

-3-

Index